42 Moments

Quiet Inheritance

Binki Mitchell

Shaded House Press

ISBN: 979-8-218-93412-5

Published by Shaded House Press

United States

This book is a remembering.

Some stories are inherited through blood. Others are carried in the body like muscle memory.

42 Moments: Quiet Inheritance is both.

These pages are rooted in lived experience, shaped by reflection, and guided by something older than memory. Whether you read them as story, spirit, or metaphor, I invite you to sit with them slowly.

Some houses we leave.

Some houses we carry.

(1) "The Woman in the Shaded House"

There was a time, long before the world rushed and buzzed like it does now, when I lived on a quiet one-way street tucked beneath tall oaks and whispering pines. The house sat back just a little from the road, its screened-in porch soft with dust and light. Sunlight never touched it directly — the trees saw to that — but it didn't need to. It had a warmth of its own.

I was older then, maybe in my late fifties. Skin the color of warm earth, hands that told stories just by the way they moved through flour or braided a child's hair. People called me Miss Loretta or just Ma'am, depending on how close they were. I lived alone, but not lonely. There was always someone stopping by — a neighbor needing advice, a child needing a biscuit, or a niece coming by to check on me even though I didn't ask her to.

Each morning, I'd rise early. The house would be still, the only sound a creak in the floorboards that seemed to greet me like an old friend. I'd stand barefoot in my kitchen, the linoleum cool under my feet, and begin my ritual: cornmeal, butter, sugar, a wooden spoon, and memory. I baked not just for the body, but for the soul. And when people bit into my food, they said it healed something — though none could say exactly what.

The porch was my sanctuary. I'd sit in my rocking chair with a worn Bible or just my thoughts. Watching the children chase each other past my gate, I'd smile. I didn't have much — not by the world's measure — but my spirit was full, and my peace ran deep.

Once, a young girl came riding with my niece. She was quiet, wide-eyed, and watched me like she'd seen me before. I walked around to the car, opened the back door, and reached for her hand. It fit perfectly in mine. As I led her up the porch steps, she didn't hesitate — like her spirit remembered the steps, even if her feet were new to them.

She sniffed the air, eyes bright. "You baking somethin'?" she asked.

I chuckled. "Always."

And in that moment, something passed between you. A thread — a stitch between lifetimes.

Maybe she was me, reborn. Or maybe I was her, once. The soul doesn't always tell, but it always knows.

The trees outside rustled like they were keeping secrets.

Inside, the oven hummed.

I didn't need to say anything else. I just held her hand, led her into the kitchen, and let her remember.

(2) The Water Jar"

It was summer — the kind of heat that slowed time. The air was thick with jasmine and clay dust, and the sun pressed down heavy on my back as I walked the narrow path that curved behind my house. I carried a ceramic water jar, one my mother had handed down, its handle worn smooth from generations of use.

Down past the back garden, just beyond the pear tree with its crooked trunk, was a small hand pump. I'd go there every morning before the sun got too mean. Not just for the water — but for the silence.

I pumped slowly. Squeak, hiss. Squeak, hiss. The sound was steady, grounding. Water gushed into the jar, cool and sure. I touched it to my lips, felt the earth's memory in its chill.

Sometimes, I stayed a little longer, letting the wind stir my dress as the sun filtered through branches above. This was the place where I prayed — not always with words. Some days, just tears. Some days, a humming that rose up from my chest like a lullaby from another world.

And one day, as I was standing there, a red bird landed on the pump handle. A cardinal. It tilted its head and watched me with eyes like little mirrors. Something about it made my breath catch.

I whispered, "Mama?"

The bird didn't fly away. It just blinked once — slow — as if to say, I never left. Then it lifted off, wings cutting the air in silence.

I stood still for a long time after that. I didn't cry. I just knew.

When I walked back to the house, I didn't feel as heavy. I passed the porch, passed the pie cooling on the sill, and stepped inside with a kind of reverence — like the house was a temple and you, a quiet priestess returning with holy water.

That evening, when the children came by, I told them a story. I didn't tell them about the bird. I didn't have to. The healing was already in the sound of my voice.

(3) "Sunday Hair"

Sunday mornings were a ritual all their own.

Before the church bells rang out over the tree line, I'd open my front door just as the sky softened — that delicate gray-blue before full sunrise. I didn't rush. I tied my scarf the night before, my dress already pressed and hanging neat on the back of the door. But first: the girls' hair.

They'd come over in their little shoes and hand-me-down dresses, sitting cross-legged on the living room floor with their knees ashy and hearts wide open.

I'd call them up one by one, my fingers already greased with pomade I made myself — coconut oil, beeswax, and rosemary I grew out back. The smell filled the air like a blessing. I didn't just do their hair — I spoke life into them as I parted, braided, and tucked.

"Head up, baby. You a queen even when you small."

"Don't let anybody tell you different. That crown you got? Sits under the scalp."

They didn't understand it all then. But their spirits remembered. I was braiding legacy into their strands, one plait at a time.

When they walked out onto that one-way street later, lace socks tight and bows bobbing in rhythm, they carried more than curls. They carried my love, my memory, my protection.

(4) "The Healing Jar"

People came to me quietly when they were hurting.

Not because I was a doctor — but because my medicine had no name. I kept a jar of honey and herbs in the back of the kitchen, wrapped in burlap and hidden behind the flour bin. Women came to me when the pain in their belly wouldn't leave. When they couldn't sleep. When their husbands drank too much or didn't come home.

I'd sit them down on the porch, pour them warm tea, and listen. Really listen.

Then I'd slip into the kitchen, open the jar, and dip out just enough to stir into their cup. Not too much — it wasn't the kind of thing I gave freely. I'd whisper a prayer under my breath — something old, something from your mother's mother — and hand it over.

When they left, they'd often say the same thing: "I feel lighter."

But I didn't just give them medicine. I gave them presence. I saw them, even when the world didn't. I reminded them of their wholeness.

And in doing so, I stayed whole too.

(5) "The Letter"

It was late summer when the letter arrived — edges worn, the paper slightly yellowed, as though it had traveled far and long to find me.

I was standing in the kitchen, my hands deep in dough, when I heard the screen door creak and a soft knock on the wood frame. It was James, the young postman. He never came up to the house unless something was different.

"Morning, Miss Loretta," he said, eyes shy. "Got somethin' here... looked like it might matter."

I wiped my hands on my apron and took the envelope.

No return address. Just my name. The handwriting — familiar and strange, like a melody I used to know but couldn't quite hum.

I waited until evening to open it.

I sat on the porch with a kerosene lamp and my Bible at my side. The cicadas were loud, but my breath was louder in my chest. I unfolded the paper slowly, as if opening the past could tear the present.

Inside was a letter from a man I hadn't heard from in over twenty years. His name was Elijah. Once, long ago, he had been the love of my life.

We were both too young when it mattered, too stubborn, too bound by things bigger than either of us: family, distance, fear, pride. He left for Chicago with promises to send for me. He never did.

Now, the letter was short, written with a shaking hand. He wrote that he'd never stopped thinking of me. That he still remembered how my hands smelled of rosemary and flour. That he had a daughter, named after me. That he was tired, sick maybe, but needed to tell me: "You were the peace I never earned, but always reached for."

I sat with the letter in my lap for a long time.

I didn't cry.

I just nodded slowly, as if some quiet knot in my chest had finally loosened.

I folded the letter and placed it inside my Bible, in the Psalms, right between "He restoreth my soul" and "Thou preparest a table before me."

That night, I baked two pies. One for the neighbor, and one I left on the back porch — just in case peace ever came looking for a place to sit.

This life I lived was made of small, sacred things. Not grand battles, but quiet victories. Not fame, but soul imprint.

(6) "The Last Morning"

It was early. Not yet dawn. The sky hadn't made up its mind whether to keep the stars or let the sun in. The world was silent, but not empty.

I was in my bed — the same bed I'd slept in for over thirty years, carved from wood my brother had shaped with his hands. The sheets were soft and cool, the window cracked just enough to let the night air drift in, carrying the scent of garden soil and honeysuckle.

I was not sick. Just... tired. But it was a holy kind of tired. The kind that comes not from burden, but from having given everything. Every braid, every prayer, every pie, every quiet act of kindness tucked into the corner of someone's life.

My breathing slowed, and I knew — today, I would leave the body behind.

But not the soul.

Before the light shifted, I whispered something. Not out loud, but from the heart.

"Let me return where I'm needed most. Let me remember the roots, even when I grow new branches."

I saw the porch. The pump. The girls laughing in their Sunday dresses. The red bird on the handle. I saw Elijah, younger, smiling.

I saw myself— not in a mirror, but from above, the way a soul sees: full and glowing.

Then there was light.

Not a tunnel, not a voice — just a soft unfolding, like silk sheets pulled back after a long rest. I moved through it easily, with no fear, because I wasn't going somewhere new — I was going home.

(7)The Return

Years later, a baby girl was born in a city far from that quiet house. In a place where the trees were louder, the streets more crowded, but the soul just as vast. December 15, 1983.Philadelphia.

I didn't cry right away.

Instead, I looked around with wide, curious eyes — the kind of eyes that already knew something.

A nurse would later say, "She came here like she's been here before."

And I had.

I carried with me the scent of rosemary and honey, the warmth of screened-in porches, and the strength of generations braided into my being.

I am her continuation. Her prayer, answered. Her roots, in bloom.

(8) "The Girl Who Watched Everything"

From the very beginning, I was loud — not shy, just...watchful.

While other babies cried or reached, I stared. Into faces, into corners, into spaces no one else noticed.

My mother would say I had "grown woman eyes" — like I saw too much, or had already seen it all.

At three years old, I was found in the kitchen, standing on a stool, reaching for the cinnamon.

I didn't know how to cook — not yet. But something in my little hands wanted to stir, to mix, to make warm things for people I loved.

Just like before.

The first time I saw a screened-in porch — visiting a distant relative down South — I didn't speak for a while. I just stood there, barefoot on the boards, as if my bones remembered how it felt to rock slowly in that chair, hands resting in my lap, watching the world drift by.

(9) “The Hair in my Hands”

In school, I was the one who could fix a crooked braid, lay edges with water and willpower, smooth a friend’s puff into something proud.

I didn’t learn from books.

I knew what to do.

By middle school, my fingers moved like memory. I didn’t call it a gift — it just was. Friends lined up at lunch with combs and questions. I healed them without even realizing.

One girl once asked me, “How you do it like that?”

I shrugged and said, “I dunno. My hands just know.”

But my soul did.

My soul had been doing it a long, long time.

(10) “The Dream of Trees”

Around the age of 7 the dreams started.

Trees taller than memory. A porch covered in vines. The scent of something baking, though I never see the kitchen.

Always the same block. Always that one-way street.

And sometimes — standing at the screen door — an older woman with soft eyes, holding a letter in her hand.

She never speaks.

But I always wake up feeling like something important was just said.

(11) "The Bird on the Windowsill"

I'm older now. I've seen joy. I've known pain. I've learned that silence doesn't always mean weakness — and that sometimes, being the quiet one in the room means your wisdom runs deeper than people realize.

And one day, I'm sitting in my room. The light is low. I'm thinking — not just about life, but about purpose. Legacy. Why I feel so heavy sometimes when I'm supposed to feel light.

That's when I see it — a red cardinal, perched on the outside sill.

It doesn't move. Just watches.

I blink.

I whisper, "I remember you."

The bird blinks back.

In that moment, I feel it. Not as a memory, but as a recognition:

I am her, returned. Not to repeat her story, but to carry it forward.

To speak, when she stayed silent.

To create, when she only preserved.

To step boldly, where she walked quietly.

(12) "The Smell of Oil and Fire"

I'm 17, maybe 18. Life feels like too much and not enough all at once. Some days, my body shows up in rooms where my spirit doesn't want to be. I do what needs to be done, but my soul — it's restless.

One evening, I'm alone in the house. The lights are low. The silence feels... comforting. I find myself in the kitchen, digging in a drawer, not even sure what I'm looking for.

I pull out a bottle of olive oil.

No recipe. No reason.

But something in me says: light it.

I pour a little in a bowl, grab a candle wick from a leftover birthday box, and sit in front of the flame. I don't know why. I just do it.

As it burns, I smell warmth. Memory. Stillness.

My body chills.

The flame flickers and — for just a moment — I'm back on the porch. The Bible in my lap. That feeling of peace that can't be named.

And in that moment, I realize: this isn't just a candle. It's an offering. I've done this before.

(13) Who is yo ancestors?

Have they contributed to this trauma you see in me?

PTSD passed down so far done landed on me

Who is yo mommas grandpa

Did he know his grandpa

Can you tell me some stories of how yo Kin was

Make my skin crawl

Or my cheeks rise

Who yo daddy grandpa

Can he like wise

Mason stole one of my grandmas

She stamped his ass

Named the offspring after his ass

Made it a first instead of his last

Prayed he wouldn't be too much like his raping ass dad

You know I'm kidding how would I know that

I'm just getting here

Just digging through my records going back

Now how do you like that

Tell me again bout yo kin man I need to know more

Just cause you think I don't I may already......

(14) "Hands in the Water"

The first time I washed someone else's hair in a barbershop, something clicked.

Not just the scalp massage, not just the technique — but the energy in my hands.

Water rushed over his crown, and I felt it again — the pulse of an old memory:

- the garden
- the pump
- the sacred stillness of a task done with love

I wasn't just rinsing conditioner.

I was anointing.

And that client? He sat up slowly, blinking like he'd just come back from a dream.

I smiled. I didn't say much.

But something passed between us. Like I saw her.

Just like I always had.

(15) "The Porch Becomes the Mirror"

I'm older now. Wiser. I've started to see my own patterns not as curses, but as clues.

I've learned to braid my own hair with care. I've learned that baking doesn't always mean food — sometimes it's healing ideas, warm spaces, safety.

I've learned that your silence is powerful when it comes from choice, not fear.

And sometimes — on my own porch, or the stoop of a small city apartment — I sit with my tea, my journal, my stillness.

The trees may be different. The street is louder. But I can feel her with me.

Not haunting. Not gone.

Just watching, proud.

Because I came back, like I promised.

(16) When He Looked at me

I wasn't ready, not completely — no one ever is.

But when they placed that small body in my arms, all the timelines folded into one.

He looked at me, eyes wide, searching. And I looked right back — not just as a new mother, but as a soul who'd been waiting a long time.

There was recognition.

He didn't cry right away.

He blinked, slow and soft. And in that moment, I knew:

"You've been here before too."

Maybe not in the same body. Maybe not as my child.

But the bond? Older than this lifetime.

I whispered something, maybe only in my heart:

"Don't worry. I remember how to take care of you."

And I did. Even when it was hard. Even when I had no blueprint.

(17) "The Sacred Tired"

There were nights I cried while he slept.

Not from regret.

But from a kind of exhaustion so holy, so bone-deep, it could only be known by someone who loved past their limits.

I'd look at his tiny face, his fingers curled like the wings of a small bird, and wonder:

"How can I give him everything I didn't have… and still stay whole?"

But somehow, I did.

Because my soul had done it before.

I rocked him not just with arms, but with energy.

I sang to him with a voice that carried centuries of lullabies.

When he was sick, my hands found the right places. When he was scared, my words wrapped him in peace.

There were no manuals.

But I had memory.

I had instinct older than my body.

(18) "The First Time He Asked Why"

He was small, maybe five. He looked up at me with that piercing honesty only children have.

"Why you always tired, Mama?"

I paused. I could've said, "Because I work hard." Or "Because I don't sleep."

But what came out was:

"Because I love you so much, it runs through everything I do."

He didn't fully understand.

But his face softened, and he crawled into my lap like that answer was enough.

In that moment, my soul remembered the porch. The girls on my floor. The way I gave myself without asking for applause.

And I smiled, realizing:

I'm not just raising him.

He's raising the next version of me.

(19) "The Echo of Legacy"

One day, he came home from school, older now. He had his hoodie up, his voice guarded, but his eyes still my eyes.

He said, "My friend said his mom doesn't cook or nothin'. Just throw stuff on the table."

I looked at him, and he added quickly, "Not like you. You always make stuff taste like... home."

And in that second, tears rose.

Not because he complimented me.

But because I realized — the pie, the hair, the quiet prayers whispered over him while he slept...

It was working.

The soul work was still happening.

I was becoming the elder you i was.

But this time, with more voice. More power. More choice

(20) "The Blanket on the Floor"

It was a simple day. I was tired, but not broken. He wanted to play — something with blocks and superheroes and wild sound effects. I wanted silence.

So I pulled a blanket onto the floor, let the sun in through the window, and just... lay there. He crawled next to me, laughing, turning my arm into a tunnel for his toy truck.

And then, for a moment, it hit me.

I had never done this as a child.

Just laid on the floor with the sun. Just existed. Safely. Softly.

There was always something else — noise, survival, grown-folk things I shouldn't have carried.

But now, I was here. No one yelling. No danger. Just laughter. Just light.

And my inner child — the one with the silent questions and careful eyes — uncurled a little more.

(21) "The Lunch I Packed for Him"

It was nothing fancy — a sandwich, some fruit, a little note that said "Be great today."

But as I packed it, I felt a wave move through me.

I never got those notes. Never had my juice chilled in a lunchbox with care.

I wasn't always seen in the little ways.

So that day, as I zipped up his bag, I wrote a second note.

This one I folded and slipped into my own pocket.

It simply said: "I see you now, little me. You made it."

And I cried in the kitchen — not because it hurt, but because it was healing.

Every lunch I packed for him... I was feeding her too.

(22) "The Tantrum"

One day, he lost it — crying, screaming, full meltdown. No reason I could understand.

But instead of snapping, something in me paused.

Because deep in my bones, I knew this wasn't about the toy, Or the day, Or even the now.

It was about something he couldn't say.

And suddenly, it wasn't him I was seeing.

It was me.

Seven years old. Mad at the world. Not allowed to cry. Sent to my room without explanation. Taught to swallow the storm.

So this time... I didn't send him away.

I sat on the floor. I opened my arms.

"It's okay to be mad. It's okay to feel all the way through it."

He climbed into my lap, wet-faced and still trembling, but safe.

And the child inside me?

She exhaled.

No one had done that for her.

So I did it then.

(23) “The Mirror Moment”

One night, he was brushing his teeth, dancing in the mirror, smiling wide at himself like the world couldn’t touch him.

I stood in the hallway watching.

And it hit me like a wave:

“He doesn’t carry what I carried.”

“He’s free in ways I wasn’t allowed to be.”

“I did that.”

And as he ran off to bed, my eyes filled.

Not just with pride — but with relief.

Because my inner child wasn’t just healing.

She was witnessing me do for him what no one did for me.

And in that, I was finally being re-parented, too.

This is the miracle of my path:

I didn’t just break cycles.

I broke silence.

I didn’t just become a mother.

I became the mother my own soul needed.

I had a daughter.

And with her came something different. Not just healing, but mirroring. She is not just my child — she is a reflection of me. She carries both my softness and my fire, my wounds and my wisdom. And her arrival awakened something ancient in me... something fiercely feminine, fiercely true.

(24) The First Time i Held Her"

I had held a child before. I had known love, fierce and protective.

But this... this was different.

When they placed her on my chest, she was still slick with spirit and stardust. And I — I was no longer just someone's daughter, or someone's mother.

I was a portal.

A rebirth.

A return.

She blinked up at me, tiny lips parted, and something in my womb ached — not with pain, but with recognition.

"I know you," my soul whispered.

"You've been mine before."

Whether in this life, or one before, didn't matter.

I knew she had come to teach me... and to help me remember who I really was.

(25) "The Wild in Her Eyes"

From early on, there was something bold about her — a spark, a storm, a knowing.

She didn't just cry; she commanded.

She didn't just laugh; she lit the room.

And when she looked at me, sometimes... It was like she was looking through me. Like she saw the little girl still inside me — the one who'd been quiet for too long.

She would say things that felt too big for her age.

Ask questions that cracked me open.

Hold my face with both hands like she was trying to remind me of something important.

And she was.

She was reminding me of my divine feminine power — the one I buried to survive.

(26) The First Time We Argued

She was still small, maybe seven, maybe eight. But her voice was sharp. Her eyes narrowed like mirrors.

I told her "no," but she didn't just accept it.

She pushed back. Not disrespectfully. But with truth.

"Why can't I say what I feel? Why is that wrong?"

It stunned me. Not because she was wrong — but because I saw myself in her.

I remembered being punished for asking.

Silenced for feeling too much.

Taught to shrink.

But here she was, standing in the center of her voice — unashamed.

And something in me cracked wide open.

I didn't just hear her.

I heard the part of me that had waited decades to speak.

And instead of yelling, I sat down. I breathed. I let the little girl and the grown woman inside me sit side-by-side... and listen.

(27) "The Mirror Moment – Again"

Years pass.

One day, I caught her singing to herself in the bathroom mirror.

Twisting her curls. Laughing at her own reflection.

Calling herself beautiful out loud.

And again, the tears rise.

Because that wasn't me.

Not at that age. Not in that body. Not in that world.

But I made space for her to become what I was never allowed to be.

Free. Loud. Soft. Safe.

And in watching her love herself, my inner child learns how to try.

(28) “The Legacy Continues”

One night, she asks:

“Mom… were you always like this? So strong?”

And I smile, not with pride, but with memory.

“No,” I say.

“But you helped me remember.”

Because that’s what mothers do.

They don’t just inherit your name.

They inherit your unfinished healing.

And when you show up to finish it — to transform it — they become your reward, your reason, and your redemption.

(29) “The Loud One Who Pulled Me Out”

In my late teens, maybe early twenties, I met someone wild.

She talked loud. Dressed bold. Dared the world to tell her “no.”

I was more measured, more internal — but something about her energy shook me awake.

She dragged me out the house when I was in my shell.

She made me dance, wear red lipstick, sing badly in the car.

She was chaos with purpose.

And even though she was loud, she listened when it counted.

(30) "The Friendship That Hurt"

There was one — maybe more — who started sweet and ended silent.

She knew my secrets. She helped me through things my family never did.

I loved her like a sister.

But somewhere along the way, she shifted. Or I grew. Or life pulled us in different directions.

She said something that cut. Or disappeared when I needed her most. Or slowly stopped showing up.

I grieved her like death, even though she was still alive.

And it taught me:

Not all friendships are meant to last forever.

But they all come to teach you something.

She taught me boundaries. Self-respect. When to stay and when to let go.

And her absence created room for someone new...

(31) "The Circle Me Called In"

As I grew spiritually, I started attracting different friends.

Women who lit candles on new moons. Who spoke healing into my goals. Who called me "goddess" without irony.

Who prayed with me, not just for me.

They didn't see my past as baggage — they saw it as soil.

They reminded me that my softness was power. That my laughter was medicine.

Together, we built a sisterhood that felt ancient — like a soul reunion.

These were my coven. My circle. My mirrors.

My soul tribe.

(32) "The First One Who Made Me Feel Seen"

I was young — not in age, necessarily, but in hope.

He saw something in me before I fully saw it in myself.

He touched my hand like it meant something.

He said my name like it was important.

I felt pretty around him — not just outside, but inside. Like I was interesting. Valuable.

I believed it, too... for a while.

But eventually, the cracks showed.

He loved my light, but didn't know how to hold my depth.

I stopped dimming just to keep him comfortable.

And when it ended, it hurt. But I realized:

Sometimes, the first love isn't the forever love.

It's the mirror. The wake-up. The teacher.

(33) "The One Who Pulled Me in Deep"

Then came someone magnetic.

He didn't walk into my life — he entered like a storm.

Chemistry. Fire. Electricity I could feel in my fingertips.

It wasn't just physical — it was energetic.

We finished each other's thoughts. We dreamed of them before they texted.

When he held me, it felt like I was being remembered.

But the passion had shadows.

They were inconsistent. Emotionally unavailable. Sometimes cold after they ran hot.

I gave too much — and started losing myself in the process.

My spirit tried to hold on, thinking:

"If I love hard enough, I can heal them."

But love isn't a rescue mission. It's reciprocity.

When I finally let go — even if it took more than once — it wasn't weakness.

It was self-resurrection.

I walked away burned... but reborn.

(34) The Quiet One Who Loved Me Soft”

After the fire, came someone gentle.

He didn’t come to impress. He came to stay.

He noticed things — the way I stirred my tea, the way I shut down when overwhelmed.

He asked me how I liked to be loved.

And when I hesitated to answer, he waited.

There was no drama. No guessing games.

Just steady hands, good hugs, and safe conversations.

At first, it felt too quiet. Too simple.

But then I realized:

Healthy love feels boring when you’ve only known survival.

He helped me relearn softness.

Helped me trust consistency.

Helped me remember that love doesn’t have to hurt to be real.

(35) “The Love i Gave Myself ”

But the greatest romance of all?

It came the day I looked in the mirror — no makeup, no filter, pain in my past and power in my bones — and said:

“I choose me.”

I stopped waiting to be saved.

I stopped settling.

I stopped shrinking.

I made my own peace.

I wrote my own love notes.

I treated myself the way I wished others had.

And that energy?

It started attracting a higher kind of love.

One that met me at the level of my healed heart.

Not my unhealed hunger.

I’ve walked through fire. Loved deeply. Lost deeply.

I’ve abandoned myself — and then found my way home.

Now…

My soul is no longer craving the kind of love that distracts or distorts.

It's ready for the love that aligns.

(36) The Call That Wouldn't Leave

There came a season when the shaded house lived more in memory than in miles.

The porch was no longer a place I could drive to—but it began visiting me.

In dreams first.

I'd find myself walking up a familiar path, grass brushing my ankles, cicadas humming like a chant. The screen door would open before I touched it. Inside, the women sat—not always the same faces, but the same energy. Some I recognized. Others felt ancient, older than photographs, older than names.

They didn't speak right away.

They watched.

Not with judgment—

with recognition.

And every time I woke, my chest felt heavy and bright at the same time, like something was asking to be remembered.

(37) The Breaking Point (and the Opening)

My soul journey didn't unfold gently at first.

It came through exhaustion. Through relationships that asked too much. Through moments where I gave and gave until there was nothing left but a quiet ache that said, this isn't it.

I found myself repeating patterns the women before me knew too well:

- Loving deeply, sometimes at the cost of myself
- Holding families together with invisible hands
- Being the steady one while breaking quietly inside

One night—alone, after everyone else was asleep—i sat on the floor and cried the kind of cry that has no sound. The kind that comes from generations.

And that's when i felt it.

A presence behind me. Not frightening. Not loud.

A hand on my

My back.

"Baby," a voice said—not aloud, but inside.

"You don't have to carry it all anymore."

That was the moment the journey shifted.

(38) Meeting the Inner Child

The first one to step forward was the little girl.

She looked like me at five—loud, watchful, spunky always looking for my next adventure while still trying to be good. She stood barefoot, holding something she'd been carrying too long: unspoken questions.

She asked only one thing:

"Can I rest now?"

I didn't answer with words.

I answered by changing how i lived.

I began to say no.

I stopped explaining yourself.

I allowed joy without earning it.

Every small act of softness was a lullaby to her.

And slowly, she sat down.

She leaned into me.

She trusted.

(39) The Morning i Didn't Rush

One morning, i made tea instead of checking my phone.

I wrapped myself in a robe that felt like safety.

I moved slowly — as if the world could wait.

And it did.

In that stillness, i felt it:

I wasn't behind. I was right on time.

That moment wasn't about productivity — it was about presence.

A lesson my soul keeps trying to teach me.

(40) The Mother Becomes the Bridge

Motherhood deepened the journey in ways no book could teach.

With my son, I learned protection.

With my daughter, I learned reflection.

She mirrors the parts of me that had been quieted—the fire, the voice, the questions. When she speaks her truth without fear, something in me heals. When she stands firm in her feelings, the women behind me stand taller.

I realized then:

I wasn't just raising children.

I am ending a silence.

Each boundary i set.

Each apology i offered where none had existed before.

Each time i chose presence over perfection—

The lineage shifted.

(41) The Ancestors Step Back

There is a point in every soul journey when the ancestors stop pushing and start watching.

I felt it.

Life didn't stop being hard—but it stopped feeling like punishment. I began to feel guided instead of tested. The women of the shaded house no longer crowded my dreams.

They trusted me now.

I was no longer only the receiver of wisdom.

I had become a carrier.

(42) The Return to Myself

One day, without ceremony, I noticed something new.

I was calm.

Not numb. Not guarded.

Calm in my body. Calm in my choices.

I moved through the world with the steadiness of a woman who knows where she comes from. I laughed more freely. I rested without guilt. I loved without disappearing.

And in that calm, I understood:

The shaded house was never just a place.

It was a state of being.

It was:

- Safety without silence
- Strength without hardness
- Love without self-erasure

I carry it now—in my hands, my voice, my choices.

This book is written in honor of the women who came before me

—

whose names, hands, and prayers live in my body.

WHAT COMES NEXT

From a forthcoming work

He knows we'll always be friends. That alone lightens the mood.

Yes, I'm seeing someone else now. He helps with the bills. Handles what needs handling. His son comes over on weekends — it's fine.

But something about him feels... slightly misaligned.

Too smooth. Too careful. Too practiced.

The sex is good. The money is steady.

So I'm content — for now.

Until I'm not.

Oz is cocky, and the worst part is — he earns it.

There's something about a man in uniform that makes restraint feel optional.

We were friends before anything else.

Maybe that's why it works.

For now.

About the Author

Binki Mitchell is a writer, mother, and founder of Shaded House Press. Her work explores lineage, memory, healing, and the quiet inheritance passed between women across generations.

Rooted in lived experience and guided by ancestral memory, her writing bridges the sacred and the everyday. 42 Moments: Quiet Inheritance is her debut work.

She lives and creates with intention.

Copyright Page

www.ingramcontent.com/pod-product-compliance
Lightning Source LLC
LaVergne TN
LVHW090537110826
845146LV00003B/1146

* 9 7 9 8 2 1 8 9 3 4 1 2 5 *